Book available in four languages:
French, English, Spanish, German, Italian.

ISBN : 9798873656769 - English Edition Paperback

How to get views on TikTok ?

Understanding the TikTok Point System:

Engagement Metrics : TikTok assigns points to various user actions, which collectively influence how the algo promotes your content :

likes	1 point
comments	2 points
reposts	3 points
watch until end	4 points
rewatch	5 points

TikTok:
The Master of Attention

The Rise of China in the World

of Algorithms

China's Masterstroke

The Chinese social media platform ,

TikTok has changed the Internet!

Be yourself

"It's no longer just an app on their phones, it's their livelihood! That's how they communicate with their friends."

TikTok, the Master of Attention
(China's Masterstroke)

Book Contents

Introduction   **PAGE 11**

Chapter 1:   **PAGE 12**

From Altavista to TikTok
Story of the Internet: From Origins to Today

Chapter 2:   **PAGE 14**

Pioneers of Online Search: Yahoo! and Google
2.1 Yahoo!: A Revolutionary Web Portal
2.2 Google: Transforming Online Search
and CPC/PPC Advertising

Chapter 3:   **PAGE 17**

The Rise of TikTok, the Dopamine of Marketing
3.1 Genesis of TikTok: China Awakens
3.2 International Expansion: TikTok
3.3 Cultural and Technological Revolution:
Endless Scrolling
3.4 Challenges and Controversies:
A Spyware for Data Collection
3.5 Influence on Generation Z

3.6 TikTok, Only 6 Years Old !
3.7 International Expansion is Inevitable, Inexorable
3.8 Growth and Global Adoption
3.9 Innovations and Unique Features of TikTok

Chapter 4:   **PAGE 21**

4 Regulatory Challenges and Adaptation
4.1 Cultural and Technological Revolution: TikTok
4.2 Challenges and Controversies: Governments Wake Up
4.3 Influence on Generation Z
4.4 Future Perspectives
4.5 The Explosive Development of TikTok with musical.ly
4.6 The Era of Short Video
4.7 Slowing Down TikTok Since 2019
4.8 Growth and Expansion
4.9 Appointment of Shou Zi Chew and Record Growth
4.10 Hacker Attacks in 2022?
4.11 TikTok Stop or Encore
4.12 Influence of Charli D'Amelio
4.13 Political Tensions and Data Security
4.14 Avoiding India's Fate

Chapter 5:   **PAGE 29**

5 Total Influence on *Generation Z*
5.1 Loyalty and Interests of *Generation Z*
5.2 Influence on *Generation Z*: Australia and Indonesia
5.3 Daily Connection and Growth in Usage Time
5.4 Demographic Evolution of Users

5.5 Tiktok vs. Metas (Facebook)

5.6 The Impact of TikTok on Social Media and Video Giants

5.7 Instagram's Painful Adaptation to the All TikTok Era

5.8 Instagram Facing TikTok: Zuckerberg Sweating

5.9 YouTube: Adapting to Stay Relevant

5.10 The Imitation of Shorts and the Response

5.11 Analysis of the Evolution and Decline of YouTube/ Instagram vs TikTok

5.12 Time Spent and Preferences of Young People
on Social Networks

Chapter 6: **PAGE 39**

Lives on TikTok & understanding the TikTok Point System

6.1 Basics of Lives on TikTok

6.2 Basic Techniques for TikTokers

6.3 Monetization Strategies

6.4 Reaching and Engaging the Audience

6.5 Engaging Interactivity Effectively

6.6 Monetization and Sharing of Lives

6.7 Advanced Strategies and Practical Tips

6.8 Practical Tips Post-campaign Analysis

6.9 The Best "Lives" of 2024 on TikTok:
From Eliza (Australia) to ADM (Algeria)

Chapter 7: **PAGE 46**

7.1 TikTok, the Brain Time Available: The Era of Retention
7.2 165 Hours per Month on Tiktok:
TikTok Swallows Your Time, Your Life
7.3 The Secret of Tiktok: The 2 Algos
7.4 Strategies for Success and Trend Analysis
7.5 TikTok as a Space for Individual Expression
7.6 Responses to Political Challenges and Government Censorship
7.7 Internal Features and Virality on TikTok

Chapter 8: **PAGE 53**

How the Algorithm Works
8.1 Tips for Affiliation and Monetization
8.2 Building Solid Trust with Users
8.3 Tensions between TikTok and Silicon Valley
8.4 Unstoppable TikTok
8.5 TikTok Surpasses Facebook
8.6 Impact and Reactions of Lobbyists
8.7 Data Security Issues and Partnerships
8.8 Approval of the U.S. Government: The Imperative of Partnership with Oracle in the United States

Chapter 9:   **PAGE 59**

March 2023: The Decisive Month
9.1 CEO Hearing and Political Implications (March 2023):
The Tension between TikTok and the Authorities

Chapter 10:   **PAGE 61**

The Future of Social Media - The Legacy of TikTok
10.1 Predictions and Evolution of TikTok:
Impact of the Lockdown and Global Deception

Chapter 11:   **PAGE 64**

TikTok as Dominator of Social Media

11.1 TikTok: The Most Downloaded App in the World
11.2 The Global Appeal of TikTok
11.3 TikTok in 2024 and Beyond

Conclusion: **PAGE 67**

Sources: *PAGE 69*

INTRO: The Dream of the Youth:
I'm a Full-Time Tiktoker

Imagine a world where ideas, cultures, and connections intersect at the speed of light. This world is ours, shaped by an endless digital web: the Internet (Inter Networks). It all started with Arpanet, the military's network, an audacious and visionary project of the 1960s. It was the dawn of a revolution, the first step towards building a global network. But this was just the beginning, a world without algorithms, a world of simple communication.

In *1989*, a genius named *Tim Berners-Lee*, working at **CERN** in *Meyrin (Geneva)*, Switzerland, added a cornerstone to this emerging edifice: HTML. This simple yet powerful language breathed life into the World Wide Web, allowing computers to communicate with each other, a scientist's dream, turning a network of machines into a universe of endless possibilities: exchange.

Then came the browsers, those magical portals to the digital world, presenting content. Netscape, launched in 1994, boldly opened this window, closely followed by the giant Microsoft with Internet Explorer, which carved out its own significant niche. It was as if, suddenly, the entire world was just a click away. 1995 marked a revolution for the first initiates, with the creation of the first websites like sunflowers.com, selling seeds worldwide. It was the ancestor of the virtual world, and the first web-focused communication agencies, like the pioneering Agence Virtuelle in Geneva, emerged. In January 1995, sending emails was not yet a common practice.

Chapter 1: from Altavista to TikTok

In the heart of this digital explosion of the 1990s, pioneers like **Altavista** and **Yahoo!** paved the way, organizing the immense chaos of information into something comprehensible, navigable. **Yahoo!** was the reference directory, and **Altavista** the hyper-powerful engine that responded to keywords, the precursor of algorithms. But the real game changer was Google, which was made the default search engine in **Yahoo!**, leading to Yahoo!'s demise. By the late 90s, **Google** was not just a search engine; it was a revolution in how we find and interact with information, with keywords, a new **Altavista**. For 20 years, there was the rise of blogs and social networks like **Facebook, WeChat**, and video engines like YouTube, which was acquired by Google. Instagram, too, was acquired by **Facebook**, as was **WhatsApp**. Everything seemed set in stone.

And now, here we are in 2024, 30 years later.
The birth of the web where no one would have bet on a Chinese company capable of dethroning the American titans and octopuses of *Silicon Valley*.

TikTok has redefined the digital landscape in record time, and nobody saw it coming. Like its predecessors, **TikTok** is not just an app; it's a culture, a phenomenon that transcends borders and generations. With its addictive short videos, ingenious algorithms, and undeniable social impact, **TikTok** is not just an entertainment platform; it's a mirror of our society, a playground for creativity, and a catalyst for change. This innovation panicked the tech brands of *Silicon Valley*. Here is its story, written with *AI*.

This book is thus an odyssey through digital time and space, from Arpanet to the global phenomenon TikTok. We explore how TikTok took over from the internet giants to become an essential Chinese cultural force globally. Prepare to dive into a fascinating journey through history, technology, all intertwined in the colorful fabric of **TikTok**, the master of your time, the master of your attention. But let us recall some stages of the life of the Internet without TikTok...

Understanding the TikTok Point System:

Engagement Metrics : TikTok assigns points to various user actions, which collectively influence how the algo promotes your content :

likes	1 point
comments	2 points
reposts	3 points
watch until end	4 points
rewatch	5 points

Initial Video Distribution : when you post a video , it is initially shows to 300 viewers, the algo checks how many points your video receives, if the video fails to accumulate 50 points, it may not be promoted further.

Chapter 2: The Precursors of Online Search

Yahoo!, Google, and Other Pioneers

Yahoo!: From Web Portal to Online Search In the mid-90s, Yahoo! emerged as a beacon in the burgeoning chaos of the World Wide Web. Founded by *Jerry Yang and David Filo*, two students from Stanford University located near Palo Alto, Yahoo! began as a simple directory of websites categorized by topics. However, it quickly transformed into an indispensable web portal, offering everything from news to messaging services. Yahoo! was more than a directory; it became a search engine by incorporating Google, the Trojan horse; it was a gateway to the internet, a place where information was organized and accessible. However, this partnership spelled the kiss of death for Yahoo!

Google: Revolutionizing the Search Engine, SEO, and CPC/PPC *(Paid Per Click)*

Then came **Google**, the brainchild of *Larry Page and Sergey Brin*, also from *Stanford University.* Launched in 1998, **Google** revolutionized online searching with its **PageRank** algorithm, which assessed the importance of web pages based on their incoming links, page freshness, content, and the famous keywords in page copywriting. **Google** not only made searching more efficient; it transformed how information was indexed and retrieved, with a minimalist design, a single logo in color, and no more portal.

With the large-scale introduction of **SEO** (Search Engine Optimization) and **CPC** (Cost Per Click), Google changed not only online searching but also digital advertising with keyword bidding and auctioning (*Bid Management System*) for sponsored links on the right side of the screen… This marked the death of Yahoo! Then came the rise of social networks around 2007, with Facebook, which remained unchallenged for about 10 years… until… the arrival of the Chinese tsunami.

The Birth of TikTok

The birth and meteoric rise of **TikTok** took the web players by surprise. This chapter will explore its origins, from its inception by ByteDance, a company based in Beijing, to its international expansion. We will cover how **TikTok**, initially launched as Douyin in China in 2016, was adapted and rebranded for the international market in 2017 as **TikTok.**

Chapter 3: The Advent of TikTok

3.1 Genesis of TikTok: China Awakens

TikTok, an app revolutionizing the world of short video sharing, originated as **Douyin** in 2016. Created by ByteDance, a Chinese tech company founded by *Zhang Yiming* using proceeds from selling an apartment he found through an algorithm, **ByteDance** began. The app was designed to fill a gap in the social media market, offering a platform for short, creative, and often musical content (like dances). <u>By 2016, the Chinese version of **TikTok** had 100 million users,</u> leading its founders to launch an international version: the idea of TikTok was born.

3.2 International Expansion: TikTok

In 2017, **ByteDanc**e launched **TikTok** for international markets, an adapted version of **Douyin** outside *China*. **Douyin**'s recommendation algorithms were extraordinary, functioning like those in financial markets. **Douyin** represented a breakthrough, collecting your reactions, time spent on videos, music, landscapes - every piece of information was analyzed. This was the model of endless reactivity. The global expansion of **TikTok** accelerated in 2018 when **ByteDance** acquired **Musical.ly**, a popular social media app among American teenagers (168 million in 2016) and French (28 million in 2016), but little known to the general public. They didn't immediately merge. Their features and user base with **TikTok** only merged in 2018. This merger was a key moment in **TikTok**'s history, significantly broadening its reach and user base with a solid foundation.

3.3 Cultural and Technological Revolution: The Endless Scrolling

TikTok introduced a new way of consuming and producing content on the Internet through a clever mix of short videos and background music. Its algorithm technology, which personalizes video streams for users based on their preferences, changed how people interact with online content: the feed is endless, with little or no keywords. Intermittent positive reinforcement is used. And as expected, in 2020, **TikTok** became the most downloaded app globally, testifying to its massive impact in the digital entertainment realm.

3.4 Challenges and Controversies: A Spyware for Data Collection?

Despite its success, **TikTok** faced several challenges when the app became too visible, too large, too threatening. Concerns about data privacy and censorship emerged, especially in the *United States*, where the **Trump** administration attempted to ban the app in 2020. However, **TikTok** responded to these challenges by strengthening its privacy policy and seeking to diversify its portfolio, but is that enough to ensure its longevity?

3.5 Influence on Generation Z: Infinite Virality

TikTok has significantly impacted *Generation Z*. The app has become a platform where young people express their creativity, share their experiences, and connect with others globally. It has also influenced music, fashion, and other aspects of pop culture, becoming a barometer of trends for the youth, setting fashion and music trends.

3.6 Future Perspectives: The LIVES

In 2024, **TikTok** continues to evolve and adapt, moving too fast for its American competitors. With the introduction of new features, such as **TikTok** Lives and integrated e-commerce *Shopping Live,* the app seeks to extend its influence beyond video sharing. It is a major player in the social media universe, challenging established historical giants. Instantaneity prevails, let's look back on its history, in detail.

3.6 Creation and Expansion of TikTok: From China to the Global Stage
TikTok: Only 6 Years Old!

After just six years of existence, the Chinese app is hot on the heels of the old dinosaurs, who did not see this rapid global success coming. In the heart of Beijing in 2012, a tech startup named **ByteDance** was born under the guidance of *Zhang Yiming.* **ByteDance**, with its avant-garde vision, quickly established itself in China's world of technology and algorithms. However, it was in September 2016 that the company changed the game with the launch of **Douyin**, the Chinese predecessor of **TikTok**, exclusively for the Chinese market. Within a year, **Douyin** attracted over 100 million users and generated over 1 billion video views daily. A record. China became a domestic test market like the USA, a future consumer market.

3.7 International Expansion is Inevitable, Ineluctable

Building on its success in China, **ByteDance** launched **TikTok** on international markets in September 2017. This international version of **Douyin** was designed to captivate a global audience while retaining the essence of its Chinese version. The year 2018 marked a decisive turning point for **TikTok** with the acquisition of Musical.ly, a popular video-sharing app among American teenagers, completely unknown in Europe. This strategic merger not only extended **TikTok**'s reach but also merged user bases, creating a unified global platform in record time - ByteDance's masterstroke.

3.8 Growth and Global Adoption

The rapid adoption of **TikTok** worldwide has been phenomenal. In 2020, **TikTok** surpassed 2 billion global downloads, with a strong presence in the United States, India (before its ban), Turkey, Russia, and beyond. In China, **Douyin** continues to dominate with over 600 million daily active users, reflecting the app's popularity and engagement. **Douyin** is expected to reach 1 billion users in China by 2025, accounting for a 75% market share.

3.9 Innovations and Unique Characteristics of TikTok

TikTok stands out with its intuitive, vertical interface, easy-to-use creation tools, and especially its two recommendation algorithms that personalize video streams for users based on their interactions (just scrolling). These innovations have not only allowed **TikTok** to distinguish itself in a competitive market but have also redefined how content is consumed on social media. **TikTok** did to social networks what the iPhone did to telephony, the thumb revolution; everything became simpler, a finger now directs the world. Variable interval rewards do the rest, becoming dopamine in its purest form.

Chapter 4:

The Cultural and Technological Revolution of TikTok

4.1 Cultural and Technological Revolution: TikTok

TikTok is more than a video-sharing app; it's a significant cultural and technological revolution, particularly for teenagers who are future adults. **TikTok**'s audience is expected to age similarly to the French radio group **NRJ**, which has remained number one since its inception in 1981, as its audience ages but remains loyal to the media of their youth. **TikTok** is on the same path but on a global scale. Teenagers of 11-14 years old today will be the users in 10 or 20 years. **TikTok** has altered how people create, share, and consume content. Features like duets, challenges, and creative filters have encouraged unprecedented interaction and creativity. Its AI-based personalized recommendation algorithm has changed how users discover content, making each experience on the app unique.

The exceptional quality of the **TikTok** application, particularly its live streaming feature, is indeed noteworthy. The fluidity and clarity of these live streams create an immersive experience for users, allowing them to not only follow along in real-time but also actively participate through interactive elements like sending virtual gifts, such as roses, which are part of **TikTok**'s unique payment system.

Moreover, the interactive nature of **TikTok** Lives, where viewers can comment and interact with the audio, transforms it into a hybrid of radio, live blogging, and citizen television. This level of engagement and real-time interaction brings a new dimension to social media, blurring the lines between different media formats and offering a more dynamic and participatory experience.

4.2 Challenges and Controversies: Governments Wake Up

As with any influential platform, **TikTok** has faced its share of challenges and controversies, particularly concerning data security and privacy, with growing government concerns about the influence of Chinese technologies abroad.

Content moderation and protecting young users from inappropriate content have also been contentious issues. **TikTok** has navigated these turbulent waters while maintaining its growth and popularity.

4.3 Influence on Generation Z

TikTok has profoundly impacted Generation Z, becoming an integral part of their social and cultural lives, in less than 6 years. The app has created a space for them to express individuality, explore creativity, and connect globally. It has influenced fashion, music, and even language, becoming a true trend barometer for the youth, and a tool for Brands.

4.4 Future Perspectives: The LIVES

Looking ahead, TikTok appears poised to continue its expansion and innovation. Looking towards the future, **TikTok** appears ready to continue its expansion and innovation, becoming a thorn in the side of governments, as **TikTok** remains a space for freedom of expression, especially in its *LIVE* streams, which are difficult to shut down and suspend in real time.

With ongoing investments in AI technology and exploring new features like augmented and virtual reality, TikTok is positioned to stay at the forefront of the social media industry.

Additionally, the company is exploring ways to diversify its revenue streams, including e-commerce and targeted advertising, while addressing regulatory and data security challenges.

4.5 Explosive Development of TikTok with Musical.ly

Following its merger with **Musical.ly**, TikTok saw a meteoric rise, becoming one of the most downloaded apps globally. Key growth factors include its sophisticated recommendation algorithm using AI for real-time personalized content, democratizing video creation with an intuitive user interface and editing tools, and encouraging viral content creation through challenges and trends.

Key Factors of Growth Recommendation Algorithm:

The heart of this growth lies in its sophisticated algorithm, which uses artificial intelligence to offer tailor-made content in real-time. Based on user interactions, this algorithm has made the TikTok feed extremely personalized and captivating. The results prove it. It's the filter bubbles. Ease of Content Creation: TikTok has democratized video creation, thanks to an intuitive user interface and a range of editing tools, such as filters (a major innovation in 2023) and special effects. These features have made content creation both accessible and entertaining: addictive, but not just for the young...

Culture of Virality: The app has encouraged the creation of viral content through challenges and trends, often associated with popular music or hashtags, thus stimulating collective creativity and engagement. #fyp #pourtoi #pourtoi #pourtoi #pourtoi A Major Technological Advance: Infinite Attention

Beyond the cultural aspect, TikTok has brought significant technological innovations. Its personalized recommendation algorithm, based on artificial intelligence, has redefined user engagement. This technology allows TikTok to offer content highly tailored to individual preferences, which increases user engagement and loyalty over the long term, what is known in marketing as retention. The retention rate for the TikTok brand is phenomenal.

Attention up to a week per month, that's the average time spent on TikTok in 2024: Time is Money, no it's TikTok.

4.6 The Era of Short Video

TikTok's impact extends beyond its platform, prompting other social media giants to adopt the short video format to maintain their standing, proving users' preference for quick, engaging, and easily consumable content.

4.7 Curbing TikTok Since 2019

In *February 2019*, TikTok faced a record fine of $5.7 million from the FTC in the US for children's privacy violations. This incident raised global concerns, leading to increased investigations and regulations.

4.8 Growth and Expansion

By late 2019, **TikTok** had over a billion users, ranking as the third most downloaded app worldwide. The COVID-19 pandemic lockdowns further boosted its popularity.

In May 2020, *Kevin Mayer*, former head of video-on-demand at *Disney*, was appointed as the American CEO of **TikTok** and COO of ByteDance, in a strategic move to strengthen TikTok's trust in the US.

4.9 Appointment of Shou Zi Chew and Record Growth for TikTok

This appointment coincided with a significant milestone for TikTok: in 2020, the app surpassed Facebook to become the most downloaded app in the world, according to sources such as Bloomberg and Reuters. The goal for TikTok was not to lose a country of 340 million potential users, as India had already banned the application.

TikTok Surpasses Google in Views

Another remarkable achievement occurred in 2021, when **TikTok** surpassed Google in terms of views, thus becoming one of the most influential and visited platforms on the Internet, according to data from Nielsen and Statista. The time spent on **TikTok** is multiplied; if we count the minutes per user or cumulative minutes, we should be talking about hours or even weeks on TikTok. It would have already been number one since 2020…

4.10 Hacker Attacks in 2022?

In September 2022, **TikTok** faced a major challenge when the hacker group AgainstTheWest claimed to have breached **TikTok** and obtained 2 billion lines of data. TikTok refuted these claims, denying any security breach.

4.11 TikTok Stop or Encore ?

In 2023, **TikTok** navigated a turbulent period with red flags raised by governments from the European Commission to the White House. These concerns, largely about espionage, led to bans on **TikTok** on professional devices of government employees.

4.12 Influence of Charli D'Amelio

In this context, **TikTok** content creators like ***Charli D'Amelio***, currently number 2, a dancer and influencer with more than 150 million followers, earn a significant amount per post, illustrating the immense economic and cultural impact of the platform. ***Charli D'Amelio***, the famous dancer and influencer, earns a significant amount per publication, estimated at about **$48,199 per post**, thus highlighting the economic and cultural impact of **TikTok**.

4.13 Political Tensions and Data Security

In 2020 and in 2023, **TikTok** was at the center of a major geopolitical conflict. The U.S. government, expressing concerns about data security amid intense anti-Chinese lobbying, threatened to ban TikTok on American soil unless the company found an American partner. This crisis terminated when **ByteDance**, **TikTok**'s parent company, chose Oracle as its strategic partner for its U.S. operations. In September 2023, this crucial agreement was approved by the U.S. government, allowing **TikTok** to continue its operations in the United States.

4.14 Avoiding India's Fate: An Absolute Ban in the US? Montana leads the way until...

The Montana Ripple: A Turning Point for TikTok

In a bold move, Montana declared a complete ban on TikTok starting *January 1, 2024*, igniting talks of a potential nationwide prohibition. However, this wave of change hit a wall when a US judge halted the ban, a decision that **TikTok** welcomed with open arms. This setback shifted the momentum significantly. By December, the US Senate commerce committee made it clear: they wouldn't be addressing **TikTok**-related legislation before the year's end.

In an unexpected twist, <u>2023 turned into the year when Congress, amidst all the buzz, seemingly overlooked the task of banning TikTok.</u>

Election Year Hesitations:

The TikTok Conundrum

Amidst the unfolding drama, the approach to 2024 election day - a pivotal election year & day: the *5th November* - adds another layer of complexity to the **TikTok** saga. Analysts speculate that Congress and the White House might steer clear of any attempts to ban **TikTok** during this sensitive period.

The reason? **TikTok**'s soaring popularity among young voters.

This demographic, crucial in swaying election outcomes, could become a decisive factor in the government's cautious stance towards the app. As the political gears shift towards the elections, TikTok's fate hangs in a delicate balance, intertwined with the pulse of the young electorate: *Generation Z*

Chapter 5: Total Influence on Generation Z

Generation Z, those born between the mid-1990s and the early 2010s, is at the heart of the **TikTok** revolution. The term "*Generation Z*" comes from the alphabetical sequence following Generation Y (or Millennials). This demographic group is the first to have grown up entirely in the digital era, which deeply influences their behaviors and preferences.

On **TikTok**, *Generation Z* finds a space to express themselves, share, and connect in a way that resonates with their innate digital identity. They spend an average of 23.5 hours per month (2020 data) on the platform, testifying to its immense attractiveness. For them, **TikTok** is not just an app; it's a window to the world, a way to connect with global trends, and a means to forge their cultural identity, a mirror of dopamine.

5.1 Loyalty and Interests of Generation Z on Instagram

In 2020, 89% of *Generation Z* (aged 18-25) in France used Instagram daily, showing strong loyalty to the platform. Popular areas for this demographic on Instagram included travel, music, wellness, and food, with increased interest in fashion and beauty compared to other social networks. These trends highlight how Instagram remained relevant for Generation Z, even amidst **TikTok**'s rise.

5.2 Influence on Generation Z: Australia and Indonesia

TikTok's global appeal is evident, with users in Australia and Indonesia spending over 29 hours per month on the platform. In France, the average is 21 hours and 24 minutes per month, indicating TikTok as the most time-consuming social network, a trend likely to continue growing.

5.3 Daily Connection and Increase in Usage Time

Approximately 90% of **TikTok** users log in daily, with the average time spent on the app increasing by 19.7% year-on-year. TikTok also leads in user spending, surpassing **YouTube, Tinder, and Disney+**, thanks to features like *Live Shopping*.

5.4 Demographic Evolution of Users

As of January 2023, 38.9% of TikTok users were between 18 and 24 years old, with a near-equal distribution in France. The average age of TikTok users is rising, indicating the app's growing appeal to a broader, more diverse audience. In the US, 41% of social media users use TikTok, with the figures rising to 67% for those aged 18-19 and 56% for those aged 20-29.

5.5 TikTok vs Metas (Facebook)

TikTok, on the verge of crossing the 2 billion user mark (2024), is challenging the META group for the top spot globally. As of January 2023, the United States hosts the largest user base of TikTok, with 113 million people. Indonesia follows with 110 million, and Brazil ranks third with 82 million users. It's important to remember that the app is banned in India; without this ban, the app would have already secured its position as the global leader of ALL brands.

These statistics demonstrate **TikTok**'s increasing global influence. Regarding **TikTok** influencers, 50.51% have between 1,000 and 5,000 followers, 29.93% have between 5,000 and 20,000, and 15.2% have between 20,000 and 100,000. The average engagement rate with influencer content is 15.86%, highlighting **TikTok**'s significance in influencer marketing, which is significantly higher than its competitors.

TikTok has become not only the dopamine for its users but also for its marketers.

5.6 Painful Adaptation of Instagram and YouTube to the TikTok Era

Instagram & Youtube Facing TikTok: Zuckerberg Sweating...

TikTok in 2024 is a Growing Giant, signaling the end of playtime for the dinosaurs of social networks, led by *Facebook*.

It's a digital tsunami! In 2023, **TikTok**, the short video app, continues to conquer the world, especially France. With its 15 million active monthly users and a potential audience nearing 21 million in France, **TikTok** has become an essential player, even within the Hexagon.

Every day, 10 million French people surf on **TikTok**, including 4.1 million young people aged 15 to 24. Each month in 2024, a crowd of 23 million internet users swarms the app in France. And that's not all: 72.2% of French **TikTokers** are under 24, with a strong concentration between 18 and 24. The youth have made their choice.

Globally, **TikTok** is a powerful war machine with 1.7 billion active users. 63% of these users are young people under 24. 3.9 billion uploads. And during the lockdown, what happened? The lockdown was TikTok's best promotional agency. An explosion of users and uses, especially among 15-24-year-olds in France, with a 27% increase compared to 2019. TikTok even became the 4th most mentioned brand on social networks... Just like that. July 2021 was a record month with 3 billion downloads worldwide, and in September 2021, TikTok surpassed the billion active monthly visitors mark. *Facebook* trembles. *Google* wavers.

Impact and Reaction of the Giants Faced with this phenomenon, **Instagram** (Facebook group) and **YouTube** (Google group) had to react urgently. Instagram launched "*Reels*," and YouTube introduced "*Shorts*," attempting to capture some of **TikTok**'s magic with these ultra-short formats, unconvincing palliatives that only delay the birth of the world number 1.

These giants had to adapt, evolve, and above all, learn to ride the **TikTok** wave, a wave that nearly wiped them out in less than four years, but their fall seems close as these behemoths struggle to reinvent themselves. Meanwhile, Instagram (thus Facebook) still reigned in 2023... at least in terms of connected users...

5.7 Instagram: Evolution and Strategic Response

In 2023, Instagram continues to mark the social media landscape in France, with more than 26 million active monthly users, ranking as the third most used social media platform, behind YouTube and Facebook. With 34.7 million unique monthly visitors in France in May 2022 and a strong presence of the 25-34 age group (45% of users), Instagram remains a major player.

Globally, **Instagram** has reached impressive milestones: 1.393 billion active monthly users in 2020 and about 2 billion by the end of 2021, positioning itself just behind Facebook and YouTube. The app was even the most downloaded in the fourth quarter of 2021.

Faced with **TikTo**k's unstoppable rise, **Instagram** launched "*Reels*" in August 2020, a feature allowing the creation of short videos, directly inspired by **TikTok**'s success, imitating what cannot be stopped. In response to **TikTok**'s ascent, Instagram introduced Reels, with more than 45% of accounts interacting with a Reel per week. Content on Reels generates 22% more engagement compared to traditional videos on Instagram, but the level of engagement is only 3% on Insta. In 2023, Instagram had more than 26 million active monthly users in France.

This innovation marks a key step in **Instagram**'s evolution, highlighting its willingness to adapt to emerging trends and meet the expectations of a young and dynamic audience.

5.8 YouTube: Adapting to Remain Relevant

 For a Little Longer YouTube, known for its long-format videos, has also felt the impact of **TikTok**. In response, YouTube launched "Shorts" in 2020, allowing users to create short videos. This feature shows how even established platforms must adapt to new trends to remain relevant. YouTube Shorts represents an attempt to capture a portion of the audience that prefers quick and engaging content, a niche dominated by **TikTok**.

These strategic adjustments by Instagram and YouTube illustrate the profound impact of **TikTok** on the social media ecosystem, compelling even the established giants to innovate and reinvent themselves. These urgent adaptations by Instagram and YouTube underscore the deep influence of **TikTok** on the social media landscape. **TikTok** has changed the way people consume online content, favoring short, vertical, and engaging videos. In response, social media giants must evolve, adopting new strategies to captivate an audience increasingly accustomed to the **TikTok** format.

TikTok is now the benchmark.

5.9 The Imitation of Shorts and Response to TikTok Format

The "Success" of YouTube Shorts

In response to TikTok's growing popularity, YouTube launched its Shorts. Although Shorts is not an exact replica of TikTok, this feature has managed to attract a significant audience, particularly among content creators looking to exploit the benefits of the short format for monetization.

YouTube's Shorts offers users a new way to express their creativity and interact with the audience quickly and enjoyably.

However, compared to TikTok, the ultimate benchmark, Shorts, as an added feature to an already established platform, faces a distinct challenge: differentiating itself in a market totally dominated by TikTok.

Despite YouTube's vast user base, the battle for screen time is fierce. Shorts must continuously innovate to maintain its appeal to users accustomed to TikTok's intuitive interface and personalized experience.

Future Prospects for YouTube (Google): Time is Counted?

The future success of YouTube Shorts will depend on its ability to offer a unique experience while leveraging the strengths of the YouTube platform. This includes the integration of monetization functions, the exploitation of vast communities of creators, and offering a user experience that complements YouTube's traditional long videos. Time is not divisible in 3D, and it seems that an entire generation has decided to use only TikTok. The statistics speak for themselves.

Adding to this, in the battle of YouTube Shorts vs. TikTok vs. Reels, YouTube, the king of videos, also decided to venture out with its own version of short-vertical videos. Let's delve into more details what you can do and specs:

- Release Date Youtube Shorts : A beta version was launched in India in September 2020, but its official launch was not until March 2021 in the United States.
- Origin Country: United States
- Video Length: up to 60 seconds

- Max File Size: 2 MB

A Few Disadvantages of YouTube Shorts:

- There is a lack of variety in videos compared to other vertical video platforms, with some tending to repeat.
- Monetization of YouTube Shorts is not possible everywhere.
- Metrics and statistics aren't very advanced.
- The Shorts video editor is basic and doesn't use artificial intelligence. AI Is the key for TikTok: Where is BART ?
- Downloading videos by an Internet user is not possible.
- Without an invitation to the creator's Fund, even great content cannot earn money.
- New accounts starting from scratch are unlikely to succeed with Shorts due to low views and interactions. However, a video may go viral, but this is infrequent.

In conclusion, if I have to choose between YouTube Shorts vs. TikTok vs. Reels, each has its pros and cons.

However, TikTok would take the first place for its **exposure and interaction**. It allows anyone to be seen and continue to grow; whether a small or big creator, an influencer, or a brand, everyone can be known and foster an active community.

5.10 Analysis of the Evolution and Decline of YouTube/Instagram vs TikTok

Among 15-24-year-olds, Instagram ranks third in terms of time spent, with an average of 19 minutes per day, behind Snapchat and TikTok. YouTube remains popular with 11-14-year-olds in France, but TikTok is quickly gaining ground. TikTok's rapid progress, particularly among 16-24-year-olds, indicates a shift in social media consumption habits, positioning it as a serious competitor to YouTube and Instagram.

TikTok's Growing Threat to Metas, Google, and Others

TikTok is rapidly advancing, especially among 16-24-year-olds, experiencing significant organic growth. This trend points to a change in social media consumption habits, with TikTok emerging as a formidable competitor to established platforms like YouTube (Google) and Instagram (Facebook). The shift in preferences among younger audiences towards TikTok's format is reshaping the social media landscape, challenging the dominance of traditional platforms and underscoring the need for continuous innovation to stay relevant, they try hard.

CHAPTER 6: Lives on TikTok

6.1 Fundamentals of TikTok Lives

The concept of Lives on TikTok offers a real-time interactive experience, allowing creators to connect directly with their audience. This feature is a powerful tool for enhancing engagement and presence on the platform. Users can follow lives globally in any language, turning every individual with a phone into a reporter. TikTok Lives cover a broad range of topics, from shopping hauls to live factory tours, giving birth to the concept of LIVE Shopping.

6.2 Basic Techniques for TikTokers To succeed in TikTok Lives:

- **Planning:** Define the theme and goal of the Live.
- **Interactivity:** Encourage questions and responses, use polls and challenges to stimulate engagement.
- **Content Quality:** Offer attractive, high-quality content aligned with the audience's interests.

6.3 Monetization Strategies TikTok Lives can be monetized through:

- **Virtual Gifts:** Viewers can send gifts that can be converted into revenue.
- **Partnerships and Sponsorships:** Collaborate with brands for product placements or sponsored mentions during the Live.

6.4 Reaching and Engaging the Audience Strategies for Attracting the Audience

Achieving a broad and engaged audience on TikTok Live requires a thoughtful strategy based on interaction:

- **Promotion Before the Live:** Use your other social media channels to announce your Live, create anticipation. Announce it when you start.
- **Attractive Content:** Choose themes that resonate with your followers and align with current trends. (News, calls to action, reflections…)
- **Interaction and Involvement:** Encourage active audience participation by asking questions and responding to comments. (Welcome them)

6.5 Effectively Engaging Interactivity

Using Relevant Hashtags: To extend your reach, use popular and relevant hashtags. (#pourtoi, #fyp, #love…) with a trendy music of the moment!

- **Collaborations:** Invite other popular creators to your Lives to reach new target audiences and broaden your audience.

- **Performance Analysis**: After each Live, review the ultimate statistics to understand what worked and adjust your future strategies accordingly (frequency, theme, duration).

- **Long Lives:** Very long Lives seem to multiply audience numbers, topic depth, and it is not uncommon to have Lives with moderators lasting over 15 hours… In France, the *Avyon* account on TikTok is a proponent of these endless Lives.

6.6 Monetization and Sharing of Lives

- **Monetization Strategies:** Monetizing Lives on TikTok is a crucial aspect for content creators:

    o **Virtual Gifts:** Viewers can send virtual gifts, which can then be converted into real revenue. From hearts worth a few cents to carousels worth 50 Euros/USD.

    o **Partnerships and Sponsorships:** Collaborating with brands for product placements or sponsored mentions during Lives.

- Sharing and Extending Reach

    o **Post-Live Sharing**: Sharing highlights of the Live on other platforms can attract a wider audience and increase visibility.
    o **Using Clips**: Extract clips from Lives and share them as regular videos on TikTok or other social networks to continue engaging the audience.

6.7 Advanced Strategies and Practical Tips Maximize the impact of TikTok Lives by:

- **Regular Scheduling:** Establish a Live calendar to build audience loyalty.
- **Quality Content:** Invest in good audio and visual equipment.
- **Interactivity:** Use interactive tools like polls, games, and Q&A sessions to increase engagement.
- **Remember** *likes* 1 point, *comments* 2 points, *Reposts* 3 points, *Watch until end* 4 points, *rewatch* 5 points.

6.8 Practical Advice for Post-Campaign Analysis:

- Understand your audience and adjust your content accordingly. (Who is the target audience?)

- Strategic Collaborations: Collaborate with other TikTokers to expand your reach.

- Post-Live Follow-Up: Engage with your audience after the Live to build a strong community. Open a Telegram or Discord to foster loyalty.

These tips are designed to help you optimize your presence on TikTok and maximize the impact of your Lives. Avoid pressure and depression, live in the present moment.

6.9 The Best "Lives" of 2024 on TikTok: From Eliza to ADM

Just Express your Real Self

To express yourself, who is number 1?

The best "Lives" in terms of audience are in US/UK countries, or note in *Australia* Miss **Rory Eliza**, who left school and now has 5 million followers, and 22,000 followers when she is in Live mode.
She posts 4 videos per day, which is 2000 videos per year.

As she says, ***"You can be yourself at the end of the day."***

Another **TikToker** is Pandorai, disabled, and pro-Palestine; his videos were deleted well before the *Israeli-Palestinian* conflict resurface last year. TikTok removes videos that it does not like under *"Community guidelines."* **BLM** (Black Lives Matter) has suffered from this. **ADM** is another TikToker, focused on history and decoding geo-political news, with 300,000 followers (on accounts deleted or reset to zero every quarter) operating from Algeria with exceptional historical and informative content, delivering 1,000 to 1,200 live followers on daily basis.

The account is often banned from France and attacked from all sides. He resists false reports, governments, and entities that want to shut him down, silence him... He resists by a clever mix of rewards sent against reports, to influence the TikTok algorithm. Just by telling the truth on social networks, ADM has become a phenomenon.

In *France* , For instance, **French House** has become essential in dance in France on TikTok at *Château d'Angers.* <u>They post four videos per day.</u> Created during the lockdown, the members are under contract (to continuously feed their account) earning 1,000 Euros for wearing a dress. 30 brands work with them, changing clothes 10 times a day. TikTokers are aware of the engagement rate; a brand pays a minimum of 1,000 Euros per TikToker, 10,000 Euros for the entire French House on stage for a video. No social network has ever attracted so many young people.

The Lockdowns have propelled TikTokers to the firmament. China attacked with two viruses at the same time, C and T. TikTok in Australia became a hit in 2020, China knows how to make hit. In October 2020, there were 2.5 million users in Australia. **TikTok** is so addictive, its algorithm is its value. Its design has absolute verticality, like its audience curve. **TikTok** recommends content for you ; you don't have to do anything, the more you scroll, the more targeted content you get, addictive; middle school students know it, they spend their lives on it. Endless scrolling for an infinite audience... That's TikTok. TikTok is like a biometric mirror that trains AI. When you film yourself, AI analyzes your face and emotions to deliver content according to your mental and emotional state at the moment. If you are relatively weak, you may be influenced by increasingly enslaving and dangerous content like diets, which reinforce anorexia, for example, for already thin people...

In 2024, "Lives" on TikTok continue to captivate millions of users, with leading influencers dominating the platform.

These content creators stand out not only for their significant number of followers but also for the quality and originality of their Lives, actively engaging their audience with varied and interactive content on thousands of themes.

From music and dance to live discussions and Q&A sessions, these Lives offer a unique glimpse into current trends and the interests of the TikTok community, which are infinite in their quest for truth, exchanges, sharing, and humanity.

CHAPTER 7

7.1 TikTok: The Era of Brain Time Availability
The Era of Retention and Attention.

For brands, TikTok has become a dream. People are addicted, spending an average of one day per month on the app, 50% of which is spent on lives that last up to 17 hours non-stop. All of this is determined by the algorithm that you guide in real-time with your scrolling. Its business model revolves around attention, identifying the vulnerabilities of human psychology to absorb as much attention as possible.

What is an algorithm? It's a software program designed to perform a task as precisely as possible, in this case, to capture your attention. The moment you open TikTok, the algorithm already decides for you, with your thumb... automatic consumption, with no conscious choice to make. This way, you train the app in real-time to release dopamine, creating a dopamine flow for you and the marketers, resulting in the highest engagement and conversion rates of social networks. What does dopamine mean to you?

The addiction to TikTok fills a void in our lives, and reduces your mental bandwidth. Your brain no longer knows how to do anything other than wait for the algorithm to decide and deliver your dose. It's like being an alcoholic, but less visible. TikTok rewires your brain and pushes you to come back, again and again. The adherence figures prove it; they are dizzying, this is what is called engagement - real chocolate bar-like dopamine.

So, take some time to garden—chocolate comes from the cacao tree—and watch nature, which is also a form of engagement. On TikTok, it is vertiginous; it's "crazy" - you're not ready for it!

7.2 -
The Dangers of TikTok Consuming Your Time & Life:

165 Hours per Month on TikTok ! = one entire week

TikTok is more than just an app for sharing dance videos. We wouldn't spend a week out of every four watching people dance.

It has become your life, or that of teenagers. The algorithm works on retention, on your attention. It knows how to manipulate your brain. It has three major impacts: you have become like the mice in the experiments of the 1950s. Those mice would press a button and receive endless rewards. Now, those rewards are in your brain – it's dopamine, and you don't even need to press anything; the AI does the job.

With every scroll of your finger, your brain releases dopamine, keeping you on the app longer, and then it's just a matter of selling your attention to advertisers.

On TikTok, the algorithm decides for you. We're no longer on Google, typing keywords into a search bar. TikTok captures your attention and reduces your ability to concentrate or make decisions about important things. With each scroll, dopamine becomes the ultimate reward for virtual happiness.

TikTok never offers any choices; it makes them for you. You guide it by scrolling. The videos are short, and the emotion is there. With every emotion, you release dopamine, like a mouse, you are the guinea pig. A very profitable guinea pig who is unaware of it.

Thus, everything else seems too slow to you. The idea of reading this book, which is 76 pages long, to learn about TikTok, seems unthinkable. Spend 90 minutes reading instead of reflecting on what TikTok really is?

The destruction of attention is underway for future generations. Concentration becomes a problem, as does focus. This is evident in the "For You" tab, where everything is served up without the need to think. But the Lives are different – more interactive, yet just as time-consuming. They lock you into a super "For You Live."

7.3 The Secret of TikTok: The Two Algorithms

Most recommendation algorithms operate based on these two technical components, which TikTok has mastered:

- ***Content-based***
- ***Collaborative filtering***

How does it work? For example, we study two users who are similar, we look at what they have watched. What User 1 has watched, and if User 2 hasn't watched it, then it is suggested to them, and vice versa. We can analyze their age or where they live... These two approaches have been exploited since 2012 by the parent company, which develops the algorithms masterfully. They know EVERYTHING about you. Don't believe me?

If you want to know what TikTok knows about you, it's simple, just ask!

To download your personal data or data from any other social networking application, go to **> Settings > Download > Request your data > Download in Json format** rather than TXT mode for easier manipulation. In a few days, you should receive the file user_data.json.

TikTok is a constant content bubble. "The Dopamine Bubble!"

.

7.4 Strategies for Success and Trend Analysis

To succeed on TikTok, creators adopt diverse strategies that take into account current trends and audience preferences. They leverage the virality of content, cultural relevance, and constant innovation. There are low-value contents, such as a bottle falling down stairs before exploding, and those that provide remarkable analysis of ancient historical civilizations.

The spectrum is broad, encompassing mainstream media-described conspiracy theories, but for there to be conspiracy theorists, there must be conspirators. TikTok poses a threat in this context, as does X (formerly Twitter), where an interview gathering 250 million views on X, or 50 million views on TikTok, is a danger to the media because its audience far exceeds theirs. Traditional media are dying, and they do not see it coming.

Tucker Carlson's new network TCN in the USA is proof of this - it's the end for cable news networks and their counterparts. ADM also delivers these historical information sessions on TikTok, operating from Algeria, where the French state can do little or nothing…against the Tiktoker.

7.5 TikTok as a Space for Individual Expression

TikTok has established itself as an essential platform for individual expression, accessible to those aged 13 and over. Beyond entertainment, this unique platform allows sharing of daily facts, access to information, and discovery of topics often undercovered by traditional media, through short videos and innovative reflections. Users explore a variety of current topics related to their interests and countries, ranging from technological innovations and patents to global news, including the automotive market, minority political movements, and, of course, the famous dances. Everything is there. **TikTok** thus offers a window to diverse perspectives, allowing its users to freely express themselves and share a wide range of knowledge and opinions. This does not please everyone.

However, governments monitor and increasingly restrict the possibility of free expression in various countries, desperately trying to categorize social networks, especially **TikTok**, into sectarian categories with new laws and decrees. Everything is planned to slow down **TikTok**. Bangladesh and Pakistan tried; they have resigned themselves. It's clear that other networks work hand in hand in sorting information with the famous fact-checkers; they are as pure as the driven snow. They do not influence any election, follow my gaze.

You will love 2024, with 30 elections taking place, from the Russian elections with results expected on May 7, 2024 (the most important date of the year), the European elections in June, and the U.S. elections on November 5, 2024. **TikTok** may be your only space for citizen information.

7.6 Responses to Political Challenges and Government Censorship:

Localizing Faced with these political and governmental challenges, **TikTok** has had to develop survival strategies to address concerns regarding data security and foreign influence over the social network. These challenges include concerns about user information confidentiality (a problem inherent to all websites) and potential political manipulation, which, let us remember, is completely absent from other social networks like Facebook. In response, **TikTok** has strengthened its privacy policy, established forced strategic partnerships with Oracle, using Trump's September 15 deadline as a shocking argument. It has taken steps to ensure greater transparency in its operations. These efforts aim to maintain user trust (who, between us, don't care much as they accept the terms without reading them) and, above all, comply with the rising demands for global regulatory controls. The excuse is to prevent the app from becoming a global leader. A Chinese app, you can't think of it, you will own nothing, but you will have a Chinese apps.

The excuse is to prevent the app from becoming the global leader. A Chinese app, you can't imagine it, you will own nothing, but you will have a Chinese app. It's a war, not just a spiritual one, but India has declared it against China. Australian data, for instance, is stored in Singapore and the USA. The fact that the app is Chinese makes it an ideal target for the USA and the West; the covert war is already underway, ready to erupt. WWIII will be on TikTok, **it's virality is unreachable.**

Chapter 8: Internal Features and Virality on TikTok

8.1 The Algorithm's Functioning The core of TikTok's virality lies in its sophisticated algorithm, which personalizes content streams based on interactions, preferences, and viewing behaviors. Content is recommended based on user subscriptions and overall engagement, such as likes, shares, comments, and the duration of watching live or "For You" feeds. To go viral, content needs to generate high engagement quickly after posting, and reaching initial thresholds like 500 or 1,000 views can trigger wider promotion.

Factors Influencing Virality

- **Engaging Content:** Videos that prompt high engagement soon after posting are more likely to be widely promoted.
- **Hashtags and Trends:** Utilizing popular hashtags and participating in current trends can increase a video's visibility.
- **Creativity and Originality:** Unique and creative content is often favored by TikTok's algorithm.
-

Innovative Features TikTok continually innovates with new features to enhance the user experience and stimulate content creation, including integrated editing tools, special effects, filters, and musical options.

8.2 Tips for Affiliation and Monetization Maximizing opportunities on TikTok:

1. **Leverage Live Shopping:** With 38.9% of TikTok users aged 18-24, Live Shopping offers real-time interaction and direct purchasing capabilities.
2. **Authentic Engagement:** Influencers with smaller followings should maintain authenticity to foster stronger engagement.
3. **Trend and Hashtag Utilization:** Staying on top of trends and using relevant hashtags can attract brand partnerships.
4. **Brand Collaboration Pricing:** Partnerships with brands that match an influencer's aesthetic and values can lead to successful monetization.

8.3 Building Trust with Users

TikTok enables brands to establish solid relationships with their community. Engaging through hashtag challenges and targeted collaborations can significantly boost sales and brand loyalty. TikTok's advertising can increase brand trust by 41%, with users more likely to remain loyal and perceive the brand as a good fit.

Global Reach and Potential

TikTok, *available in over 152 countries and 76 languages*, offers brands a global user base to target. International brands can particularly benefit from the platform's reach, with Live Shopping poised to revolutionize purchasing and distribution methods.

8.4 The Future of Marketing on TikTok

TikTok's marketing model ; **THE DOPAMINE MARKETING**, is evolving, driven by user curiosity and the ability to engage users with captivating storytelling and interactive content. Successful brand examples demonstrate the platform's power in boosting visibility, engagement, and ultimately, sales. As the platform continues to grow, its potential for brands to connect with a global audience becomes increasingly evident, making it an essential tool in modern marketing strategies.

TikTok creativity program in 2024

The **TikTok** *Creativity Program*, a new BETA initiative, **offers creators the chance to earn significantly more** than the original Creator's Fund. While the Creator's Fund typically provides 4 to 5 cents per thousand views, this new *Creativity Beta Program* can offer upwards of 1 USD or more per thousand views. Eligibility for this program is restricted to creators in the *US, UK, Brazil, France, Japan, and Korea.* Additional requirements include being 18 years or older, having accumulated 100,000 views in the last 30 days, and possessing over 10,000 followers. An example is fighting.focus, a channel in the UFC niche, which consistently garners no less than 100,000 views per video and generates upwards of 10,000 USD per month.

Chapter 8: TikTok's Internal Features, Virality, and Its Relationship with Silicon Valley

8.3 Competition and Tensions Between TikTok and Silicon Valley

In September 2021, TikTok achieved a remarkable feat by becoming the most downloaded app on the App Store, surpassing giants like YouTube and Facebook in global downloads. This success indicated a shift in economic power towards China, suggesting a future where global economic and financial dominance could move to China by 2032. In response, Silicon Valley has been shocked into creating short-form content formats, trying to limit TikTok's expansion and protect American corporate interests.

8.4 Unstoppable TikTok

TikTok's rise, not being from Silicon Valley, challenges the long-uncontested hegemony of the tech hub and opens new perspectives in the tech and social media world. TikTok's popularity demonstrates its unstoppable nature, reshaping the competitive landscape in the technology industry.

8.5 TikTok Surpasses Facebook

In 2020, TikTok exceeded Facebook in terms of user time spent on the app, with users spending an average of 21 hours per month on TikTok, a significant increase from the previous year. This rise has caused a shockwave in Silicon Valley, especially among American tech giants.

8.6 Impact and Reactions from Lobbyists

The rise of TikTok has triggered a strong reaction from established companies in Silicon Valley. Alibaba and Aliexpress were early warnings of China's rapid learning curve in tech. TikTok's rapid progress, being outside their traditional ecosystem, posed a direct threat to their dominance in the social media sector. This led to increased lobbying efforts and strategies to limit TikTok's growing influence.

8.7 Data Security Issues and Partnerships: The Oracle Partnership in the US

The partnership with Oracle in the US was a crucial turn for TikTok, aimed at ensuring data security and addressing US government concerns. Oracle's role as a technical and trust intermediary ensures that user data is managed safely and in compliance with US legislation.

8.8 US Government Approval : 15th September 2020

In September 2020, the US government approved the partnership, allowing TikTok to continue its operations in the US. This decision marked a commitment to data security and opened the door for closer collaboration with American companies.

8.9 Global Tech Companies and Data Security

This partnership set a significant precedent for global tech companies operating in the US, demonstrating that data security and national sovereignty concerns can be addressed through strategic partnerships with trusted local companies. This dynamic has since influenced how other tech companies approach data security challenges in different countries.

The Oracle partnership was a crucial step for TikTok in the US, signifying its commitment to data security and willingness to collaborate with local players. It also highlighted the challenges global tech companies face regarding data security and national sovereignty.

Chapter 9: March 2023, A Decisive Month for TikTok

9.1 CEO Hearing and Political Implications (March 2023)
The Tension Between TikTok and Authorities

March 2023 marked a pivotal moment for **TikTok**, particularly in the United States and France, regarding its dealings with global political authorities. TikTok's CEO, Singaporean *Shou Zi Chew*, endured a challenging 5-hour session on Thursday, March 23, 2023, facing a barrage of questions from US Congress members. *Shou Zi Chew* committed to hosting all data related to **TikTok**'s 150 million American users on Oracle's servers in Texas, but this failed to convince a particularly hostile Congress. Discussions centered around data security concerns and alleged ties between **TikTok** and the Chinese government. Though the hearing did not result in a total ban of TikTok, it marked a new phase in the platform's scrutiny by US authorities.

United States Hearing: The Threat of a Ban
In the United States, President *Joe Biden* signed a law in January 2023 prohibiting the download and use of **TikTok** on federal government employees' devices. Consequently, TikTok was banned in the House of Representatives and the Senate.

Hearing in France in March 2023
In France, a Senate investigative committee examined **TikTok** on *March 8, 2023*, due to concerns over murky ties between the platform and Chinese authorities, as well as TikTok's inadequate compliance with French law. The hearing of TikTok's CEO in France highlighted the need for strong measures to further regulate the platform and ensure the protection of French users' data. Following the US, France also banned TikTok for its personnel.

Political and Regulatory Implications

These hearings raised significant questions about the political and regulatory implications of TikTok's global expansion. They shone a light on the challenges faced by governmental authorities in regulating an international digital platform and the ongoing concerns over data security and connections with the Chinese government. The decisions made following these hearings will have lasting consequences on the future of TikTok in these countries.

The hearings of TikTok's CEO in the United States and France in March 2023 highlighted escalating tensions between the platform and political authorities. These events have major political and regulatory implications and underscore the challenges of regulating global digital platforms. The outcomes of these hearings will significantly impact TikTok's future in these nations.

Source: French Senate Report - Commission d'enquête sur l'utilisation du réseau social TikTok, son exploitation des données, sa stratégie d'influence

Chapter 10: The Future of Social Media -

TikTok's Legacy

10.1 Predictions and Evolution of TikTok: Impact of the Lockdown and the Global Deception

The year 2020, marked by the global lockdown in response to the pandemic, significantly impacted TikTok's explosive growth. Particularly from March 2020, TikTok and China saw a spectacular rise. A notable effect of the lockdown was observed in the US, UK, and Spain among children aged 4 to 14. During March-April 2020, time spent on TikTok caught up with YouTube. In the US, the average daily time children spent on TikTok increased by +116% to 82 minutes, with similar increases in the UK (97%) and Spain (150%). This demonstrates the massive engagement of young users on the Chinese platform.

Exceptional Engagement on TikTok

Engagement is a key factor in TikTok's success. Over 73% of monthly users open the app several times a month. In the US, user engagement increased in the previous year, with frequent users accounting for 22.6% of total users. For TikTok celebrities with followers ranging from 100,000 to over 10 million, average engagement rates can exceed 22%.

The User War: TikTok vs. Meta

TikTok's future looks very promising, with predictions indicating it will reach 2 billion users by 2025 at the latest. The competition will be fierce between China (represented by TikTok) and the US (represented by Meta) at all levels. The US is expected to double its user base from 100 million to 200 million, strengthening its presence on the Chinese platform.

Approximately 37 million of these users are from Generation Z, surpassing Instagram's Gen Z audience in the US.

Time Spent on TikTok: An Eloquent Statistic

The time spent on TikTok is remarkable and continually increasing. **On average, users spend 24 hours per month on the app, while the most dedicated spend over 72 hours, even up to 165 hours per month.** Children, in particular, spend an average of 75 minutes per day on TikTok, compared to ONLY 17 minutes on Facebook and 40 minutes on Instagram.

TikTok as a Product Search Platform

For product searches, 30% of Gen Z members prefer TikTok. While older generations and millennials lean towards YouTube, Instagram, and Facebook, **Gen Z prioritizes TikTok**. This means brands targeting a younger audience should actively engage on TikTok, share useful content to stimulate purchases, and collaborate with influencers to build trust and increase brand awareness and sales.

TikTok's future is promising, with continuous user growth and unmatched dominance in time spent on the app. Its competition with other platforms, especially Instagram and Meta, is intensifying. TikTok could become a leading player in the social media realm. Its success largely relies on exceptional engagement and popularity among Generation Z, making it an essential platform for brands aiming to reach a young audience. The era of TV ads is over; long live TikTok.

Chapter 11: TikTok as the Dominator of Social Media

11.1 TikTok: The Most Downloaded App Worldwide

TikTok has cemented its position as the unrivaled dominator of social media by becoming the most downloaded app in the world in 2021, 2022, and 2023. With over 1.9 billion downloads, <u>TikTok surpassed Facebook and Instagram as early as 2021</u>. This remarkable achievement has been sustained since 2020, despite its ban in India, where Facebook claims 2 billion users, including 1.1 billion in India. <u>Without India, Facebook would have been relegated to second place since 2020 behind TikTok</u>. In the fourth quarter of 2021 alone, TikTok recorded over 170 million downloads, with nearly 20 million from the United States. These figures demonstrate TikTok's enduring appeal, not just in the U.S. but globally, indicating its ability to maintain its leadership status in the social media world year after year.

TikTok's Resilience Against Challenges

TikTok's notable characteristic is its resilience in the face of political efforts to annihilate it. Trump's attempt to ban it due to security concerns, accentuated by an incident involving ticket purchases for an Oklahoma convention, didn't hinder its growth. Even the ban in India, a significant market, couldn't shake TikTok's dominant position. Instead, TikTok continued to grow in other international markets with a strong and captivated user base. Its ability to overcome obstacles and adapt to changes in the social media landscape is a key reason for its ongoing success.

11.2 The Global Appeal of TikTok

TikTok has become a crucial platform for a global audience. With millions of users worldwide, TikTok offers a space where users can create, share, and discover content in an entertaining and engaging way. Its appeal crosses borders and cultures, making it a global phenomenon.

11.3 TikTok in 2024 and Beyond: Sparking Curiosity and Creating Engaging Contributions

As TikTok continues to dominate social media, it is evident that its influence will only grow. Current trends indicate that TikTok will remain a dominant force in the social media industry, attracting new users and offering opportunities for creators, brands, and influencers worldwide. The app remains a catalyst for change and a key player on the global digital stage.

TikTok has successfully established itself as the undisputed leader in social media, surpassing its competitors in downloads and user engagement. Its global popularity and ability to overcome challenges make it a dominant force that will continue to shape the future of social media. **TikTok is here to stay, and its influence is set to increase over time.**

Conclusion: TikTok, the Social Media Revolution

In conclusion, **TikTok** has taken the social media world by storm, becoming much more than just a platform for sharing videos. This social media revolution has captured our attention, creativity, and even our curiosity, showing no signs of slowing down.

With **TikTok**'s parent company, ByteDance, valued at over $250 billion, the prospects for TikTok's domination are more than promising. The ambitious goal of surpassing giants like Facebook and Apple by 2032 no longer seems like a fantasy, but a progressing reality.

TikTok's story is marked by rising stars like **Charli D'Amelio,** who has amassed 152 million followers, and **Khabane Lame, <u>the new number one on the platform with 162 million followers in 2024</u>. Khabane Lame** has leveraged TikTok as a springboard to promote products like Samsung, showcasing the undeniable power of the platform, with the capability to reach 50% of Americans in just a 15-second video.

TikTok has also paved the way for a micro-influencer strategy, with impressive engagement rates of 18%, far exceeding the norms established on other platforms like YouTube (1.65%) and Instagram (3.8%). In other words, TikTok is the ideal playground for content creators and brands seeking an engaged audience. After just 5 years of existence, the master of the world is Chinese and named TikTok, much to the chagrin of Westerners and Americans.

Ultimately, **TikTok** has carved a place in the hearts of the connected world. Its cultural impact, rapid growth, and ability to be a game-changer in the social media world make it an unstoppable force.

So, what does the future hold for this social media sensation? Only time will tell, but one thing is certain: **TikTok** has already left an indelible mark in the history of social media with its unique interactivity and algorithm.

The verdict is clear. **TikTok** is already number 1 in the hearts of the connected. <u>TikTok is now the Internet.</u>

China has won.

Welcome to 2032. 4 points you read until the end !

Christophe Paroni

Thank you to everyone who contributed to this book. Gratitude.

Sources (until 31st December 2023):

1. Cnet: *TikTok already outdated? Hoop, Yubo, Twitch, Discord, Houseparty: the new apps for teens*
2. TikTok, key figures in 2019, 2020 in France and worldwide: *Digimind Blog*
3. Forrester Research: How The COVID-19 Crisis Is Affecting Consumer Behaviors In France, April 2020
4. Top brands in social media conversations during and after 2020 lockdown: *Digimind Blog*
5. Digiday Pitch Deck October 2018, November 2019, and 2020
6. Blog Du Moderateur: *Official website*
7. Médiamétrie and Médiamétrie//NetRatings – Global Internet Audience – France – October 2018 and 2019 – Age 2 and older: *Médiamétrie*
8. Médiamétrie /NetRatings – Global Internet Audience – France - January 2018 and October 2019 - Age 2 and older. Daily audience composition when brand exceeds 0.3M of VU per day
9. Médiamétrie and Médiamétrie//NetRatings – Global Internet Audience – France – October 2019 – Age 2 and older – Daily coverage France – Subcategories Blogs/community sites + Messaging
10. Agence Heaven #BornSocial 2018, 2019, and 2020
11. Médiamétrie and Médiamétrie//NetRatings – Global Internet Audience – France – October 2019 – Age 2 and older - Subcategories Blogs/community sites + Messaging – Average daily time per individual 11b. Médiamétrie and Médiamétrie// NetRatings – Global Internet Audience – France – October 2020– base age 2 and older – Daily coverage –category social networks + Messaging
12. Diplomeo Study. Web and social media practices among 16 to 25-year-olds. *Diplomeo 2021 Diplomeo 2020* 12b. International Federation of the Phonographic Industry (IFPI) study, October 2021

13. *AppTrace: App analysis (a) TikTok lawsuit news: TikTok Newsroom (b) Europe reaches 100 million users milestone: TikTok Newsroom*
14. *SensorTower Blog: Official website 14b. SensorTower Blog July 2021*
15. *Newsweek: TikTok users surge amid COVID-19*
16. *Sensor Tower's Q2 2020 Data Digest: Sensor Tower*
17. *SensorTower Blog: Official website 17b. SensorTower Blog 2021 and TV Australia 17c. Sensor Tower Store Intelligence Data Digest Q4 2020. Sensor Tower Store Intelligence Data Digest Q3 2021.*
18. *Globalwebindex, 2019 18b. Kantar TGI Global Quick View Report 2020 18c. TikTok Newsroom September 2021*
19. *App Ape Lab: Analysis*
20. *Kleiner Perkins*
21. *Qustodio Study: Official website 21b. Adweek-Morning Consult Study May 2021*
22. *App Ape Lab 2021.2022: Analysis*
23. *The Global Unicorn Club: CB Insights Review*
24. *TechCrunch: 44% of TikTok's all-time downloads were in 2019 24b. Wall Street Journal, June 17, 2021: ByteDance's annual revenue*
25. *Sensor Tower Blog: [Top-grossing apps worldwide June 2020] (https://sensortower.com/blog/top*
26. *The Guardian, 31st December 2023 (https://www.theguardian.com/technology/2023/dec/31/us-tiktok-ban-federal)*

Discover the books on awakening by Christophe Paroni.

<u>From the same author (in French)</u>

PCR, *Covid-19 La Supercherie Planétaire (ed. 2020)*

CO2, *Du Pass Sanitaire au Pass Co2, Le Grand Bullshit (ed. 2021)*

<u>From the same author , Christophe Paroni (in English)</u>

TIK-TOK : *The Master of Attention (ed. 2024, available in FR/EN/ES/DE)*

2024 *Mirage : TRUMP , Rigged Election & The Inevitable War*

UFO : *The Fabric of our Reality. (ed. 2023)*

ICT : *Mastering Market Algos (ed.2023)*

ICE : *Everything is Illusion (ed.2023)*

WAR : *The War over Power : Energy Conflict in the Age of Putin Fueling the Fire : Putin, Energy and the Principe of WWIII (ed. 2023)*

BUD : *A croak in the Brew : Go woke, Go broke.*

AI : *The New Internet - Chat GPT*

9: HACKING NUMBER 9 : The Magic of 9

The Vibrational Self : *I'M Enough* -
27 chapters for Enlightenment & Abundance

TESLA : *Revolution on Wheels : Unstoppable*

www.ingramcontent.com/pod-product-compliance
Lightning Source LLC
Chambersburg PA
CBHW062248290526
45794CB00006B/2463